Bristol

Clive Hardy

When I was asked whether I'd like to write an introduction and some picture captions for this evocative and timely book I must say that I had some misgivings.

For wasn't I just a Johnny-come-lately to this fascinating and ancient city. After all I'd only been here thirty years and the idea was to cover half a century of Bristol life. What did I know about those twenty difficult post war years when the still sleepy city was struggling to find a new role for itself after a thousand years of being in the front line of England's maritime history?

On reflection I found that I knew a lot more about those times, than I imagined. My work in the city both as a newspaper librarian and researcher enabled me to delve deeply into the past and to re-discover much about two lost decades.

Looking back on my time in Bristol I can recall many experiences lost to the present generation, but which now seem just like yesterday. I remember my first sounds of the city – such as being rudely awoken each morning by the urgent hooting from Charles Hill's shipyard in a still working city docks. It was a call to start work for the workers but for me it meant time to get my head off the pillow. It was far better than any alarm clock.

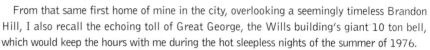

From that same first home of mine in the city, overlooking a seemingly timeless Brandon Hill, I also recall the echoing toll of Great George, the Wills building's giant 10 ton bell, which would keep the hours with me during the hot sleepless nights of the summer of 1976.

Coming new to the city I well remember my first encounter with its people. At the Easton based works of Masson, Scott, Thrissel engineering where I worked for a while, I was surrounded by friendly, but inquisitive, much related Bristolians. Conversations, conducted in the soft "Bristolese" accent that I was soon to grow so used to, would be peppered with strange phrases, such as "He'll end up in Barrow" (the local mental hospital I later discovered) and "She's just gone up the Feeder" (the canal that 'feeds' water from the river Avon into the floating harbour or docks). These were all very mysterious sounding places to me then, in those early days.

My co-workers were intrigued to know exactly what I was doing in their fair city, far from family and friends, a Brummie in self imposed exile. For Bristol was then still, despite its long history, a very inward looking and insular place. My colleagues could never have imagined that within a few years many of the old established firms, started by Bristolians and run for and by them, would go to the wall, or that "London" accents would soon begin to fill Broadmead as home counties families relocated to the West with their insurance companies.

I soon discovered how different those Bristolians could be, despite living in a smallish city. Enclaves such as Clifton, Bedminster or Fishponds, each had their own little worlds, lives of their own. The divisions were even strong enough years ago for the city to decide to support not just one, but two soccer clubs.

Above all I discovered city fathers who once had the foresight to safeguard Bristol's wonderful open spaces, such as the Downs and Ashton Court estate, desperately searching for viable use for the once bustling but now run down floating harbour. Building motorways over it and filling it in were just two of the imaginative options! Thank goodness neither actually happened.

In the past decade I've watched amazed as the city has virtually re-invented itself, with people queuing up to buy expensive dockside homes even before they are built. I've watched as once humble homes, like the Victorian railway workers terrace house I bought in Totterdown for a now unbelievable £7,000, top the £100,000 mark. New hi-tech industries and offices continue to spill into Bristol to replace the old firms, keeping the city both solvent and vibrant.

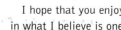

The new cafes, bars and clubs (and even the old dockside pubs where you used to be able to go for a quiet drink) seem to be ever full and people have returned to the city centre which just a few years ago seemed devoid of life after eleven at night.

I hope that you enjoy this Golden Jubilee book, looking back on a lifetime of change in what I believe is one of the country's most fascinating cities.

Gerry Brooke, Bristol July 2002.

Bristol

Contents

Around the City Centre

For our opening chapter we take a look around the city centre to see something of the changes physical, economic and social, that have take place since 1952.

With just one or two exceptions we have concentrated on the area bounded by St Augustine's Parade, The Haymarket, Bond Street, Temple Way, Temple Meads station, Redcliffe Way and Commercial Road. The Floating Harbour is included in the chapter The Maritime Dimension.

During the Second World War, British Restaurants were opened in every town and city in the country. Their aim was simple: it was that even with rationing in place, people would have somewhere to go where they could get a meal at an affordable price. This is the British Restaurant that once stood at the bottom of Park Street. The picture was taken in 1957. Note the tower of St. Marks, the Lord Mayors Chapel, now hidden from view.

College Green and the bottom of Park Street from the Council House, June 1952.

The Council House moat
was put to use on 4 March
1953 for what was billed
as the Oxbridge and
Camford boat race.

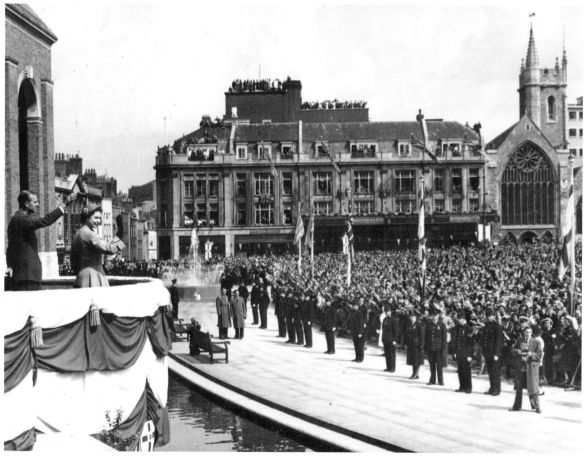

Queen Elizabeth and the Duke of Edinburgh acknowledge
the crowds gathered on College Green. 17 April 1956.

5 December 1958. Queen Elizabeth was in the city to inaugurate the subscriber trunk dialling service (STD) by placing a direct call to the Lord Provost of Edinburgh from the central telephone exchange. Bristol's STD system was the first in the UK to become operational.

The Old Tramways Centre on a rain-swept winter's evening in 1952.

The Centre especially illuminated to celebrate Queen Elizabeth's coronation 1953.
What a contrast with todays concrete mess!

The Centre prior to its Millennium makeover: when Broad Quay, which runs past the old Bristol & West building, was still open to traffic and there were grassy banks and flowers. The Centre in this picture owed much to its redevelopment in 1938 when the River Frome stretching alongside St Augustine's Parade was covered over.

Work on the new headquarters building for the Bristol & West Building Society at Broad Quay was proceeding at sufficient pace in September 1967 for the builders to announce that they hoped to "top out" before the end of the year and have it ready for occupation by mid-1968. The building however soon gained the reputation of being one of the ugliest in Bristol. In October 2000 developers Grosvenor Estate and Beaufort revealed plans to demolish the eyesore and replace it with a "metropolitan" glass-sided tower that would vary from five to 20 storeys and stretch over the buildings on Marsh Street and Broad Quay.

In April 2002, political editor Ian Onions wrote that despite missing a crucial deadline Bristol's proposed £200million supertram scheme could still be saved. Back in the 1980s there was a £38million project to run a metro (similar to that on Tyneside) on the abandoned British Railways Portishead branch with a terminus at Wapping Wharf. Later schemes were to link Bristol with a number of places including Weston-Super-Mare and Bath. By 31 March 2002, Bristol and South Gloucestershire councils were supposed to have submitted a joint supertram scheme to the Government but had got themselves bogged down over its northern terminus. Bristol favoured Almondsbury even though this would mean tunnelling under the M5. South Gloucestershire wanted to use Cribbs Causeway. Theo Wood, spokeswoman for the Government

Office for the South West said: "The deadline is not a final one for the submission of the scheme." However while local politicians squabble, the Government's ten-year transport plan which allows financial provision for about 25 light rail/tramway schemes, is attracting proposals from cities throughout the UK, and a number have been given the green light. Time is not on the councillors' side.

The junction of St Augustine's Parade and Colston Street.
11 September 1956. Bristol Omnibus Co. offices were
still to be found on the Centre.

The Lord Mayor's coach
and escort lead the way to
St Stephen's for a civic
service. 14 April 1957.

Today the Christmas Steps is one of the city's gentrified areas, attracting large numbers of visitors. Our picture dates from one of its more run-down periods.

Taken from Montague Street, looking in the direction of the Royal Infirmary. The site was developed in the 1950s for the city bus station.

St James Square was Bristol's second, and probably finest Georgian square, its houses famed for their unique shell porches. One side was destroyed during the Blitz and by September 1964 what was left was under threat from Copthall Holdings' Cumberland Street, Bond Street development.

In April 1968 Transport Minister Barbara Castle announced funding for Bristol's urban motorway scheme The Parkway. The first stage of the £16.5million motorway was for a dual carriageway three miles long to replace the hard-pressed B4058. The second stage comprised the £7.5million elevated section between Muller Road and Ashley road. Our picture is from work on the final stage: the section that would bring the M32 to the fringes of Broadmead.

The Carpenter's Arms in The Horsefair in July 1953. George's beers had been a part of city life since 1788 when Philip George bought a brewhouse, malthouse and warehouse. The strengths of George's beers were something of a local joke: it was said that its weakness was due to them simply bottling water from the Floating Harbour.

The Horsefair in October 1953. The arrows indicate the approximate location for the new Jones & Co department store.

The Armada pub and Henry Jones flour factory (where self-raising flour is said to have been invented) in the Broadmead. George's remained a family business for 150 years and at its height owned 900 pubs and a brewery at Counterslip. It was sold to Courage in the 1960s. By 1999 only one of George's brands remained in production and even this was under threat with Courage's decision to end brewing in the city. This picture was taken in July 1953. Note the excellent reflection of the Moggy 1000 in the shop window on the left.

A view of what in the Bristol of 1953 was the city's new shopping centre. This picture of Broadmead was taken from the top floor of the old Evening Post building.

In June 1982 the 'To Let' signs were going up along Broadmead following a massive hike in rents. For thirty years or more many retailers had enjoyed fairly static rents and now their landlords were catching up in one go, forcing many small independent shop owners to relocate or give up altogether.

Taken in April 1954 this is the view along Fairfax Street from Merchant Street. The Church Army Hostel, a last hope for many a man down on his luck, was demolished to make way for redevelopment.

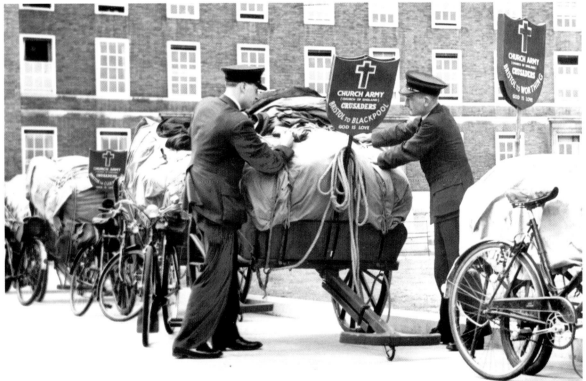

The Church Army prepares for their annual summer crusade to resorts around the country. The two members pictured here would soon be heading off for Blackpool. Allowing for meetings along the way, their journey would take about one month.

Fairfax House, the Co-op's multi-level department store was Bristol's answer to the Bermuda Triangle. It had in effect three ground floors and no matter which entrance you went in by, it was almost impossible to get out the same way. The floors were numbered on the American system, first storey, second story and so on. The first could be entered from either Fairfax Street or Merchant Street. The second was entered from Newgate Street: the third storey from Union Street. The building housed a 300-seat Exhibition Hall: it also had the Thomas French Bar, which wasn't the place for a pint, but where you bought your curtain hooks and rails. There was however the Bristolian Coffee Bar, designed to represent British Rail's new Bristol Pullman Train. It had train windows and doors, but lacked the stale sandwiches so beloved of railway passengers. It was demolished in 1988 in order to make way for the Galleries Shopping Mall.

The blitzed ruins of St Peter's Church stands proudly in
what in 1977 were newly landscaped grounds, having
recently been grassed and planted with trees. To the right
of the church stands the Co-op's ill-fated Fairfax House.
The Bristol United Press building is in the bottom left, by
the Old Market roundabout. Bottom right is the tallest
office block in the city, Castlemead, at 225 feet.

It is September 1987 and the International Continence Society is on at King Street's Theatre Royal. This wasn't one of the Bristol Old Vic's usual offerings: they had diversified into conferencing in order to generate additional income.

All that remains of Fairfax House are a few mounds of rubble. Work on levelling the site continues as it is prepared for the construction of the Galleries complex. August 1988.

Taken in January 1991. The £120million Galleries shopping centre development is nearing completion, the opening scheduled for the following July.

Taken on 20 May 1952 at the mayor-making ceremony in the old Council House, Corn Street. In April 2002 during the run-up to the English local government elections, it was stated on a BBC Radio 4 programme that the average age of councillors was 56 years. No change there then.

Archaeologists from Bristol Museum at work on the escape and supply tunnel that connected Bristol Castle with the harbour. Despite its ruinous state the castle was pressed into service during the Civil War. The Journals of the House of Commons for 2 March 1647 states that garrisons were to be maintained here and at the great fort but all other installations were to be abandoned. The Calendars of State Papers for 15 April 1653 show that the Scotch and Irish Committee were to consider making an order for the castle's demolition. The next time the castle is mentioned in state papers is on 3 October 1655. The wording suggests that demolition had in fact been carried out.

One of the Council's acts of vandalism was perpetrated in the 1930s when a road was cut across the historic Queen's Square. This picture was taken in March 1991, when plans were already taking shape to restore the Georgian square to something approaching its former glory. Closed to traffic in 1993, a £3.8million bid was made to the National Lottery in 1997 for funds to aid restoration, a further £1.2million being provided by the council and private enterprise. The plans included ripping up the roadway, installing a car parking permit system, re-routing buses, floodlighting at night, landscaping, seating and litterbins, rebuilding boundary walls and re-siting, the Grade 1 listed statue of William III.

St Nicholas Church and Bristol Bridge from the top of Robinson's building. This was one of the old gateways into the ancient city.

In February 1986 the Evening Post reported that the £16million modernisation programme to turn the Courage brewery into one of the most modern and efficient in the UK, was on target for completion during 1987. In May 1999 we were reporting that the brewery was to close before the end of the year and that one of the city's most famous names – George's, might be killed off. Courage responded. Production of Courage Best, Courage Directors and George's would continue: but in Yorkshire. The site is at present being redeveloped as high quality housing and offices.

Though Bristol has lost much of its manufacturing base, it has become a major centre for insurance and banking. In this Temple Street picture from 1981 we see work underway on the foundations of London Life's prestigious £11million headquarters building. It vacated the offices in 1997 due to a fall in business.

Old Market from the Stag and Hounds. A part of Bristol's history and one of the city's oldest taverns, it was here that the Pie Poudre Court used to meet on market days to settle disputes between traders. The court dated back many centuries, but in its latter years only the opening and closing ceremonies took place. It was finally discontinued in the early 1970s.

Tony Benn served as the MP for Bristol South East for 33 years, apart from a break between 1960 and 1963 when he was forced to leave the Commons after becoming the 2nd Viscount Stansgate on the death of his father. Benn refused the title, campaigning vigorously for the right to disclaim it. Even though he was debarred, Bristol South East voters continued to re-elect him. With the passage of the Peerage Act (1963), he won the right to relinquish his title and take his seat once more.

August 1988. A £2million scheme to widen both a stretch of Temple Way and Temple Bridge was on schedule for completion the following January. The picture was taken from the roof of the Bristol United Press building. In the foreground are the offices of Clerical Medical. We can also see the tower of the Temple Church, once a preceptory of the Poor Knights of Christ: better known as the Knights Templar. Over to the left is the headquarters building of London Life.

A floodlit Temple Meads station. January 1989.

British Rail's Blue Pullmans were the first trains in the UK to be equipped with full air conditioning and the first to run in fixed-formation sets. The first of these trains were put to work on quality higher-speed limited stop services between Manchester and London. Additional sets being built so that similar services could be operated to Birmingham, Bristol and Cardiff.

Bristol East signalbox was advanced technology when first commissioned in the 1930s. Forty years later, British Rail's Western Region's £4million resignalling scheme of the Bristol area resulted in a new signalling centre, controlling 117 route miles, being opened at Temple Meads. The centre controlled locations as far away as Taunton, Bradford-on-Avon, Chippenham, Badminton, Severn Tunnel, Charfield and Severn Beach.

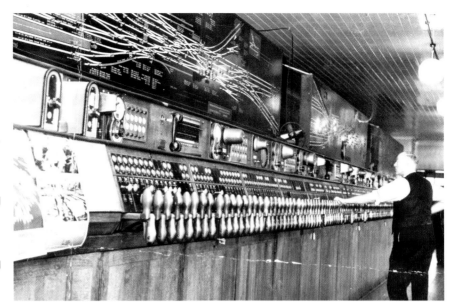

Before the Second World War the Bristolian was timed to cover the journey to and from Paddington in 100 minutes. Following nationalisation timings slipped, though there were days when echoes of former days were heard. On 28 April 1958, the steam locomotive No7018 Drysllwyn Castle covered the 117.6 miles between Bristol and Paddington in 93 minutes 50 seconds, and on one occasion No 6018 King Henry VI, reached a top speed of 102.5mph through Dauntsey, between Swindon and Chippenham.

British Railway's Western Region carried on at least one old Great Western Railway tradition: doing their own thing. So it was with dieselisation in the 1950s. Assistant general manager H H Phillips initiated a programme to use hydraulic transmission for the region's main line diesel locomotives. Pictured here on the Bristolian is a Swindon-built 2300hp Warship class loco: a scaled down version of the German Federal Railway's V200 class. For a short period the Warships hauled the Bristolian to the old Great Western Railway 100-minute schedule and several records exist of speeds of between 102 and 105mph being attained by these engines. However, the region's chief civil engineer soon imposed a maximum of 90mph: later reduced to 80mph by the chief mechanical engineer, due to problems with the locomotives' bogies.

Railway fan Jamie Harvey (6) became the proud owner of a nameplate formerly carried by an Inter City 125 power car and the first prize in an Evening Post competition which was won by his dad Michael. With Jamie is his sister April (4).

After lying unused for 28 years, the Victoria Street railway bridge was finally dismantled as part of an ambitious £500,000 scheme to transform the Temple Meads area. The bridge, which had once carried the railway line to Wapping Wharf and the city docks, was erected in the early 1960s, replacing an earlier one. Yet on 6 January 1964, the eastern and central sections of the Harbour Railway were closed, the track lifted, leaving the bridge both abandoned and hardly used.

One of Bristol's hidden treasures is the man-made Redcliffe Caves, the grill-covered entrances to which can be seen at Redcliffe Wharfe. There have been numerous schemes to reopen them, but in 2002 they remain inaccessible to the majority. Just how far the labyrinth extends is open to speculation. Some believe they extend to Knowle and Brislington. What is known is that of the 20 or so acres of caves under Redcliffe, 80 per cent is at present physically inaccessible as the system was severed in 1868 when a tunnel for the Harbour Railway was driven through the network. The last use the caves were put to was as a storage depot for council highways equipment such as road signs. They have been used for location filming in several TV series.

Taken from the tower of St Mary Redcliffe in 1955. The view is looking towards Temple Meads station. Standing somewhat prominently in the top left background is the former Great Western Railway covered goods terminus: one of the largest ever built by the company. Another interesting feature is the caravan sales yard. During the early to mid 1950's caravans were actively marketed throughout the country as a viable, and cheaper, alternative to bricks and mortar. The railway line disappearing off the picture at bottom right is the old Harbour Railway.

St Mary Redcliffe, Redcliffe Wharf and the houses of Redcliffe Parade. The replica of explorer John Cabot's ship 'The Matthew' was built on the wharf between 1994 and 1996.

Redcliffe, July 1989. An excellent view of St Mary Redcliffe, one of only two parish churches in England to have stone vaulting. The church owes much of its magnificence to the generosity of Bristol's merchants in general and to William Canynge the elder (died 1396), and William Canynge the younger (died 1474) in particular. The spire stands 285ft high: the interior length of the church is 240ft and 117ft across the transepts. The site is still beleagured by major highways despite plans to change the road layout.

Bristolians show what they thought of the Poll Tax. Introduced by an arrogant Thatcher Government in the face of warnings that it would be unpopular with the majority of people. Just how unpopular is shown by the fact that within two days of its introduction into England and Wales (1 April 1990), Michael Heseltine was given the job of reforming it.

The new-look Centre following its controversial £4million revamp funded by the Millennium Commission. The fountains, lights and pedestrian promenade weren't to everyone's liking: many felt that Bristol had been robbed of one of its few green areas: the council having destroyed a part of the city's heritage. Green and pleasant have given way to grey and uninviting.

The Centre in April 2002. Work on remodelling began early in 1999 and was finished with eleven days to go to Millennium Eve when thousands of revellers crowded the area to mark the arrival of the 21st century. However it wasn't long before things began to go wrong. The fountains didn't work properly for months and were only fixed when the council threatened legal action. The cobbled surface was difficult to walk on – especially for the elderly, disabled and mothers with pushchairs, was cause for concern and complaint.

Princess Diana chats with the late Sir John Wills, Lord Lieutenant of Avon, during her visit to Bristol in June 1990. While in the city she paid a flying visit to the Bristol Drugs Project in Guinea Street, Redcliffe to see for herself something of the work done there.

In February 1999 it was officially announced that Morse Code would no longer be the principal form of communication at sea for maritime emergencies: spelling the end of the SOS distress call. The code had been replaced by a new global satellite system. Even so the Cabot Tower would continue to flash out the message "Cabot Tower, Brandon Hill, Bristol" from dusk to dawn. In 1994 keen-eyed boy scouts and anyone else knowing their dots from their dashes would have spotted the message actually saying "Cabot Tower, Brendon Hill, Bristol."

A Jubilee jamboree for more than 500 residents at The Friendship, Knowle. Landlady Marlene Short and a crew of loyal helpers organised the party, which saw the closure of streets leading from the pub.

Give us a twirl. Taylor Martin just five months old and the great-great grandson of The Friendship's landlady, already knows how to party.

We're out to celebrate. It's street party time at South Croft, Henleaze, as friends and neighbours celebrate the Queen's Golden Jubilee. June 2002.

Party veterans Joyce Britton (left) and Sue Jackway at the Valley Road, Mangotsfield, celebrations. Joyce and Sue had become the street's party organisers. The pair's party for the Queen's Silver Jubilee proved to be such a hit with the locals that they went on to run similar bunfights for Charles and Diana's wedding, the 50th anniversary of VE Day, and even England's 5-1 victory over Germany. Their Golden Jubilee party included a fancy dress parade, music and entertainment as well as outdoor games and races.

Residents of Ashley in Kingswood raise a cheer, and a flag, at their Golden Jubilee street party.

Taken from Easton-in-Gordano and looking along the route of the M5, across the Avonmouth Bridge, to Junction 18. On the far bank to the right of the motorway are the houses of West Town Road, Barrow Hill Crescent and Watling Way. To the left are the streets of Avonmouth with the industrial estates, smelting works and chemical plant beyond.

In this chapter we start at Avonmouth, drop down into Clifton and then swing sort of northwards towards Filton for a look at Bristol Cars and BAe.

From there we head for Eastville, Kingswood, Barton Hill, Bedminster and Whitchurch before turning for Portishead. Once again Avonmouth Docks, Royal Portbury and Portishead Docks are included in the chapter The Maritime Dimension. Enjoy.

8 June 1977. The kids of Saltmarsh Drive, Lawrence
Weston, enjoy their Silver Jubilee bunfight.

During the early months of 1985 the residents of Avonmouth must have been thinking that someone somewhere didn't like them all that much. Our picture from April of that year shows firefighters tackling the fifth chemical leakage to hit the place so far that year: the second within a month. This particular incident involved the leakage of a large quantity of ammonia gas from the Union Cold Storage plant, Avonmouth Way. The nearest homes were just 300 yards away in Jutland Way.

Commonwealth Smelting No4 Complex, Avonmouth. Zinc smelting came to Avonmouth as a direct result of the outbreak of the Great War. Prior to 1914 Germany was the main centre for smelting Australian zinc ore: the war naturally changed that, the British Government moving quickly to establish the National Smelting Co. In 1967 the plant was refurbished and equipped with what was then the world's most advanced, and largest, zinc blast furnace. Avonmouth remains the UK's main zinc production facility.

There has been a white-painted tree at the Henleaze end of the Downs for well over one hundred years, yet to this day no one really knows why, or when the tradition started. The first tree was felled in 1951 to make way for a traffic roundabout. Tree number two, an elm, pictured here in 1972, was chosen as a replacement. This had to be felled soon after when it was found to be suffering from Dutch elm Disease. Tree number three, a lime, was planted in 1975.

Autumn on the Promenade. The Downs, 13 October 1957. The ancient elms died of
Dutch Elm Disease in the 1970's but have since been replaced.

Throughout the 1950s and 1960s Bristol Zoo remained a major tourist attraction. It was still a period when private car ownership was comparatively rare: the zoo was easy to reach by bus or train and was the ideal day out for people as far away as Tewkesbury, Gloucester, Swindon and Taunton.

Ape house overseer Mike Colbourne and four-year-old Jeremiah take a well-earned banana break during a walk round the zoo. Jeremiah was the 15 gorilla born at Bristol: his dad Daniel being the first.

Best remembered for fronting some of the pioneering television wild life programmes that were specifically targeted at children, Johnny Morris is in his element feeding the penguins.

Clifton Cathedral took two and a half years to complete at a cost of £800,000. A bold and somewhat controversial design from a team of designers led by local architect Ronald Weeks, it was won an award from the Concrete Society for being the best concrete building completed in 1973. Concrete was cast in wood to create a grained effect and the building has a cocoon of expanded polystyrene and external granite cladding. Known locally as the concrete tuning folk, it can accommodate 900 people.

A scene from the consecration
of the Cathedral Church
of Saints Peter and Paul
in 1973.

Across the rooftops of Clifton with Victoria Square in the foreground,
28 March 1956. A lot of this area had become run-down, very different
from the high prices of today's properties.

Maggs & Co's furnishing store in Queen's Rd, Clifton. Damaged during the Blitz, it wasn't until August 1954 that work began on a £250,000-rebuilding programme. Behind the dray you can see what at first glance looks like an occupied ground floor. It isn't. Someone came up with the rather clever idea of fronting the bombed-out part of the building with a row of display cases.

HM Prison, Horfield. In March 1987 it was described in a Commons report on prison medical services as "gaunt, ill equipped and overcrowded." The prison was caught up in the riots of 1986 when a prison officers' overtime dispute and the unsatisfactory conditions in which inmates were being held, led to unrest.

24 February 1953. Members of the public read the notices confirming the execution of Miles Giffard. He was hanged following his conviction for the murder of his father at Porthpaen, Cornwall.

Bristol Parkway on the South Wales – London route was one of British Rail's success stories. With easy access to both the M4 and M5, Parkway was planned from the start as a commuter station and offered free parking for 1000 cars. This picture, taken in 1976, shows what was then British Rail's fastest train, the 1629hrs Reading to Bristol Parkway. The Inter City 125 was timed to cover the 75.8 miles at a speed of 95.7mph.

8 August 1977. Guides and Brownies from Chipping Sodbury await the Queen's arrival at Filton. During her visit to Bristol the Queen performed the official ceremony giving the name of Royal Portbury to the West Dock.

Filton from the air. The village of Charlton was obliterated
in the late 1940's in order that the runway could be
extended for the Brabazon project. This gave Filton one
of the longest runways in the world and the former
Brabazon assembly hall gave Filton the infrastructure
needed for it to become the UK's leading centre for the
production of aircraft.

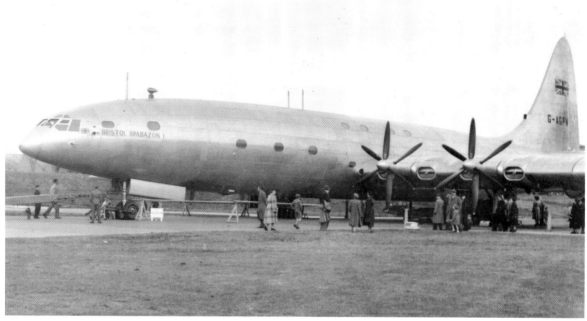

Brabazon 1 photographed on the 12 September 1952. By the time the plane first took
to the air in September 1949, it was already out of date: too slow (top speed 230mph):
too stylish for the up and coming economy/mass market type of airline operation.
Along with her sister she was broken up. Though they were white elephants, the design,
technical and engineering experience gained during their construction proved invaluable
during the development of later generations of large airliners.

Piloted by A J "Bill" Pegg, the Bristol Aviation Co chief test pilot, the first Britannia aircraft lifts off from Filton
for her maiden flight. Powered by four Proteus turbo-props, each developing 3780 equivalent horsepower, Britannia had a
maximum range of 5600 miles. The wing span was 140ft: height 36ft 8ins; length 114ft and track 31ft. Her maximum
all-up weight was 140,000lb. BOAC had already shown confidence in the design by ordering 25 aircraft. In those
days, these aircraft carried 50 passengers on long-haul flights, 100 on short-haul.

9 April 1969. BAC's Concorde chief test pilot, Brian Trubshaw (left) and deputy chief test pilot John Cochrane, prepare Concorde prototype 002 for its maiden flight from Filton to Fairford.

With nosecone drooped to improve the pilot's view during take-off and landing, a British Airways liveried Concorde is seen here at Filton. The plane was one of the great technical achievements of the 1960s – a joint effort between BAC and Aerospatiale of France. Powered by four Olympus engines, Concorde cut the flight time across the Atlantic by more than half. But at a cost. With accommodation for only 100 passengers and expensive to operate, only national carriers British Airways and Air France placed orders. The Soviet Union's TU-144 was very similar in design and took to the air three months before Concorde.

BAC Concorde workers
protest over possible
redundancies.
February 1976.

In 1946 the Bristol Aeroplane Co established a car division. From the very beginning cars were built by hand and by restricting production to a handful of vehicles per week, the company soon gained a reputation for exclusivity and reliability – a reputation that survives to this day with the Bristol Blenheim 3. Pictured here is the 405 saloon, prior to it being exhibited at the 1954 Earl's Court Motor Show. This is Bristol's only 4-door model to date. The front end was similar to the 404 'gentleman's express' sports coupe: the extra legroom in the 405 achieved through a longer wheelbase. It was powered by a Bristol 2-litre 100 B-2, developing 105bhp at 5000rpm. Some 43 drophead coupe versions of the 405 were built: the bodywork by E D Abbott of Farnham.

In 2002 Bristol is the only luxury car manufacture in the UK that is wholly under British control. In the 1970s the company finally broke into the potentially lucrative US market, switching production to a left-hand drive version of the 412S2 convertible-saloon. Chairman and managing director Tony Crook was able to announce that the firm had sufficient orders from the States to keep the firm going for a year.

Football League secretary Alan Hardaker (right) and Bristol Rover's vice-chairman Ian Stevens discuss proposals to bring speedway to Eastville Stadium. After his tour of inspection Hardaker told the Evening Post that "Every praise is due to Bristol Rovers for finding an extra way of raising money in these hard times. But we have made it clear that speedway must not be allowed to interfere in any way with Football League fixtures..." How times have changed.

The beginning of the end for old Easton. It is 1959 and the residents of Twinnell Road move out, their homes scheduled for demolition. Their close-knit community was about to be sacrificed to the alleged name of progress: new roads and redevelopment.

Barton Hill in November 1972. By the end of 1952 much of Barton Hill had been declared a development zone: the answer to its rundown, inadequate housing was to be ten tower blocks. Bristol was to be the first city outside London to build 15-storey flats. The Lord Mayor, Alderman F G W Chamberlain, officially opened the first, Barton House, in June 1958. Described by one member of the housing committee as "An adventure in 20th century, or even 21st century living." The flats themselves had large rooms, the luxury of a bathroom, and a toilet you didn't have to share with the neighbours. Latest plans announce their demolition!

Summer in the city. Fishponds Lido offered a pool, lake and sand. It would almost certainly be classified as a health and safety nightmare in our nanny state of 2002. If you don't believe me go and find out just how many pages of A4 paper have to be filled in for an acceptable risk assessment on an office pencil sharpener. The Lido is now a lake surrounded by new housing – no swimming allowed!

Founded as G B Britton in 1876, the UKS Group factory at Lodge Road, Kingswood, closed its doors for the final time in December 2001. It brought to an end the city's once booming boot and shoe industry, which in the 1930s employed 10,000 workers. By 2001 only 130 were left. Now even their jobs were being lost, victims to cheap imports and falling orders.

In order to maintain a UK manufacturing base, production was being transferred to one of Totectors' factories following a merger.

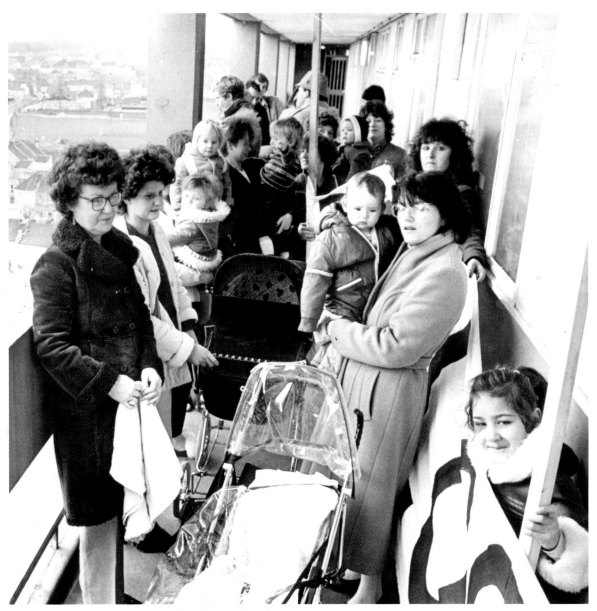

Architects, planners, economists, sociologists, social workers and the like saw tower blocks as the answer to all the country's postwar housing problems. They were totally wrong. Developments like Barton Hill were equivalent of small towns, but they lacked amenities. Nowhere for kids, no place to play. When lifts broke down people in wheelchairs were trapped in their flats: mothers struggled up flights of stairs with pushchairs, children and shopping. This picture was taken in January 1983 when mothers, concerned for their children's welfare, decided to take direct action. Having been ignored by Council officials, they made their feelings public by draping a 70ft banner along the 13th floor walkway, 'The Blocks Are No Place For Children.'

The opening of the Great Western Cotton Factory in 1838
was to be the catalyst that transformed Barton Hill from
rural community to industrial suburb. Within two years of
its opening the mill was employing over 1000 workers.
During the American Civil War, the Federal Navy's
blockade of Confederate ports starved Britain's mills of
their essential raw material. To make matters worse,
machinery used for processing American cotton, couldn't
handle Indian cotton. Some mills re-equipped, others
waited it out, and many closed for good. Despite cotton
famines, insufficient capital and economic cycles of boom
and bust, the Great Western survived for 80 years, until
sold for conversion to Western Viscoses Artificial Silk
Mills. The new owners pumped £400,000 into the business
and though it was a technical success, it proved a financial
disaster. The mill was sold in 1936 to local businessman
Douglas Parker who carried out extensive improvements
to create the Barton Hill Industrial Estate.

Class II, Sussex Street Primary School, St Philips, 1953. Back in the 1950s playtime was the time to run around and let off steam. Not any more. These days schools face the prospect of being sued almost at the drop of a hat. Did you know that in 2002 some of the playtime activities that are now banned in many schools include: conkers, marbles, hide and seek, running around, skipping, tag, even swapping cards (i.e. Pokemon).

Christmas party time at Sussex Street Nursery & Infants School, 1955.

Yet another nail in the coffin of the city's manufacturing industry with the closure in 1983 of Bristol Commercial Vehicles and the loss of 530 jobs. Situated in Bath Road, Brislington, BCV had been building buses since 1912, its customer base expanding to include the likes of South Africa, India and Rhodesia. By the 1980's it was in the clutches of British Leyland, it's end well and truly assured.

Walter Street, Southville, April 1959. One of Will's tobacco factories looms large at the end of the street.

Some areas of the city had more than their fair share of flooding during the 1960s. Here the residents of Bedminster's somewhat appropriately named Bath Street, begin the task of salvaging their household effects following flooding in June 1968. Hopefully flood alleviation schemes of the 1970's mean that it should never happen again.

Bedminster from the air. 17 May 1988.

Louise Joy Brown from Bristol made history when she was born at Oldham General Hospital on 25 July 1978. She was the world's first test tube baby. To celebrate her fifteenth birthday, Louise invited every other test tube youngster in the UK to a party at Thorp Park, Surrey. More than 1000 turned up. As Louise rightly said "This is brilliant. If my mum hadn't had the treatment, these children may never have been here." Her birth was recently listed as among the 100 most important events of the last century.

W D & H O Wills' Hartcliffe complex stood in 56 acres of landscaped grounds, the factory itself covering 13 acres. Construction began in 1971: cigarette production starting three years later. Hartcliffe replaced the company's older factories at Bedminster and Ashton. Hartcliffe turned out 400 million cigarettes and 150,000lb of handrolling tobacco every week. The factory closed in 1991.

Packing machines at work at W D & H O Wills' Hartcliffe.
Their 13 acre factory was at one time the biggest in Europe.

John Harvey with his wife Liz (centre) and children James, Julia and Mary at a dinner to celebrate the 200th anniversary of the famous drinks firm. John, the great-great grandson of the firm's founder, to the guests that Harvey's had chosen the 200th day of the year for the dinner as the exact date of its coming into existence was unknown. The first Harvey joined the firm in 1822, but it didn't get the famous name until 1871.

The Bottling Hall at Harvey's Whitchurch factory. The company lost its independence in 1962 and now belongs to Allied-Domecq.

In 1949 the go ahead was given for work to start on the building of Portishead B power station on a site between the A station and the dock. Full commissioning would take ten years: the nearby Albright & Wilson plant would in fact absorb much of the new station's generating capacity. The railway station already occupied part of the site. It had to go. British Rail chose a location about half a mile to the south to build a new station, sidings and signalbox: officially opening it on 4th January 1956. Our picture shows the old station about six months after abandonment by British Rail.

One of the many long
vanished landmarks you
will find in the pages of
this book. This cottage
once stood next to the
Portishead branch, deep
in the Avon Gorge.
26 May 1952.

British Rail's new station lasted only eight years. Falling revenue and increasing maintenance costs, combined with competition from buses and growing private car ownership, spelt the end of the Portishead branch. Here on 7 September 1964 the last passenger train departs for Bristol.

There were plans in the 1980s to incorporate the Portishead branch into a metro network, but nothing came of it. 2002 saw a revival of rail traffic with the branch being reactivated and upgraded for the running of freight traffic out of Royal Portbury.

The power station has now been consigned to the pages of history. In August 1982 sightseers gathered in eager anticipation to watch the demolition of the second of its 7,000 tonne chimneys. At a similar event the previous September when the station's other chimney had bit the dust, debris showered surrounding houses. This time however everything went according to plan.

Portishead, 22 June 1973. The city of Bristol had owned the manor and much land in the area since as early as 1616, but commercial development didn't start until the 1820's. The last 40 years have seen a housing boom.

The residents of Pouldon Road, Portishead, bring out the bunting for their celebrations marking Queen Elizabeth's Silver Jubilee. June 1977.

The Princess Royal with Avon and Somerset chief constable David Shattock during her visit to the constabulary's new headquarters at Portishead. The building wasn't without its critics. In 1991 angry councillor John Daw branded the £30million headquarters as a disgrace and a waste of money. "Is it any surprise the police complain about being short of money when they build a headquarters more like a stately home? It looks more like J R Ewing's mansion in Dallas with its ornate stone pillars and wrought iron gates."

That's Entertainment

It goes without saying that during the period covered by this book Bristol was a major venue for all manner of entertainment and to cover it in any meaningful detail is a book, possibly a CD and a video in its own right.

The most famous personality of all was Archibald Leach of Horfield, though he is better known to most of us as Hollywood legend Cary Grant. He was already an established international film star before 1952. However Bristol was where Peter O'Toole made his debut as a professional actor. The showboat Old Profanity is still (2002) moored in the Floating Harbour.

This former Baltic trading vessel was brought to Bristol by Bonzo Dog Doo-Dah Band front man and all round eccentric Vivian Stanshall and his wife, the novelist Pamela Ki Longfellow, and offered Bristolians some outstanding alternative theatre. In the world of music The city played host to just about every major act of the 1950s and 1960s including Billy Fury, Marty Wilde, Cliff Richard, Joe Browne, Eddie Calvert, the Beverley Sisters and the Cougars: the list is endless.

During the Swinging Sixties just about every UK act that appeared on Top of the Pops played at Bristol. Though not on a par with Liverpool and Manchester, Bristol has produced a number of bands that have made it into the charts.

By the time he appeared at the Bristol Hippodrome in 1960 rockabilly guitarist Eddie Cochrane had clocked up a string of hits of which 'Summertime Blues' and 'C'mon Everybody' have become classics. After the performance he stayed overnight, leaving the following morning with his girlfriend, the singer-songwriter Sharon Seeley, and fellow rocker Gene Vincent for Heathrow. At Chippenham the car smashed into a lamppost after a tyre burst. Cochrane was killed and Seeley and Vincent badly injured.

Moving on about 20 years and we come to Bananarama. Formed in 1981 by Keren Woodward, Sarah Dallin and Siobhan Fahey. Their first record was 'Ai A Mwana,' which failed to chart, but was heard by Terry Hall of Fun Boy Three. He then arranged for the girls to back his group's offering of 'It Ain't What You Do, It's The Way That You Do It.' Fun Boy Three then returned the honours by backing Bananarama's 'Really Saying Something.' This single enjoyed a ten-week run in the UK charts, reaching number five. The rest they say is history.

TV and film production companies have used Bristol either as the setting, or for location shooting, From the BBC's Shoestring (starring Trevor Eve) to the feature film Some People, which starred Kenneth More and David Hemmings. In 1975 animators David Sproxton and Peter Lord set up Aardman Productions. Their early work included a series of shorts for the children's TV programme Take Hart: featuring a clay character called Morph. During the 1980s they expanded into advertising work, but things really took off in 1985 with the arrival of Nick Park. He had been invited to join Aardman to finish an animated film he had begun while a student at the National Film and Television School. Using clay models, it featured a cheese-loving inventor named Wallace, and his dog Gromit. One of the biggest film hits of the summer of 2000 was Chicken Run. Financed by Steven Spielberg's DreamWorks: it was animated by Nick Park and filmed at Filton. And, if there is anyone out there who isn't aware of the plot, Chicken Run was inspired by the war film The Great Escape but is set on a chicken farm.

One of Bristol's own first-generation rock 'n' roll bands were the Comets (Vic Thomasson, Pete Creed, Andy Perrot and Mike Creed). Before breaking up in the late 1960s they had supported such acts as Joe Brown, Gene Vincent and Billy Fury. They reformed as a seven-man line up in 1984, including three of the original members.

Formed in London in 1981, Bananarama became one of the UK's most successful female groups. Keren Woodward, Sarah Dallin (both originally from Bristol) and Siobhan Fahey, had 23 Top 40 singles and four hit albums during a nine-year career. Siobhan left in 1988 and went on to further fame with Shakespeare's Sister. In February 2002, Sarah and Keren performed a selection of Bananarama hits at the Astoria, Tottenham Court Road, during the 20th anniversary show at GAY in London.

A season of lunchtime theatre gets underway on the Old Profanity in May 1984 with the extravagantly-costumed Kooney Wacka Hoy. Taking part were Bristol Old Vic Theatre School students: Geoffrey Owen, Anthony Howes, Lisa Bowerman, Julia Ford, Corliss Preston, Andrew Black, Ian Crowe and Michael Corbridge.

Michael Jackson fans camped all night outside the Hippodrome in the hope of getting tickets for Wacko's 1988 Wembley concert. The box office sold its allocation of 2000 tickets in less than two hours.

When Scottish and Newcastle breweries attempted to call time on jazz nights at the Old Duke in King Street in 1994, they unleashed upon themselves a storm of protest from musicians, jazz lovers, the City Council and the Evening Post. Bristol South MP Dawn Primarolo even tabled an Early Day Motion in the Commons, calling upon the brewery to rethink its position. Despite being one of the city's top tourist attractions, the pub wasn't taking enough money – too many listening, not enough boozing. The brewery changed its mind and jazz continues to be played. Pictured here are landlord John Stone (retired January 1995) and a few of the regulars. Bristol had always had a thriving jazz scene centred on the old 'Ship' pub at Redcliffe and 'The Granary' at Welsh back.

Shirley Bassey enjoys the moment. She received rapturous applause from her fans after giving a sensational open-air concert at the Lloyd's Bank amphitheatre in June 1993. On top form Shirley belted out the hits as only she can.

A local landmark is consigned to history. After more than half a century, the canopy of the Hippodrome is torn down. July 1965. A new replica canopy is now in place.

In July 1973 the Bristol Old Vic announced that Peter O'Toole had agreed to appear in three of the autumn season's productions. O'Toole was no stranger to Bristol: back in 1955 he had made his first professional appearance here. O'Toole had gone on to international stardom, so his agreeing to appear was a major boost to the theatre. Between 3 October and 18 December, he would play the title role in Tchekov's Uncle Vanya: play D'Arcy Tuck in the Ben Travers' farce Plunder, and King Magnus in Shaw's The Apple Cart.

Restoration comedy time at the Bristol Old Vic with a scene from The Country Wife. Left to right are: Victoria Wicks (Mrs Squeamish), Phillipa Gail (Lady Fidget), Stephen Yardley (Mr Horner) and Ingrid Lacey (Miss Dainty Fidget).

Bristols most famous son, Archibald Leach, better known to most of us as Cary Grant. He is seen here on one of his regular trips to the city to visit his relatives. He would always tip off 'Post' photographer, Jack Garland, when he was about to arrive in town.

Bristol has been used for location filming by a number of TV and film companies. Here a part of Avonmouth Docks was transformed into Calcutta for the filming of the feature comedy Foreign Body. Starring Trevor Howard, Warren Mitchell and Victor Bannerjee, it followed the adventures of an Indian who travelled to London to seek his fortune.

The queue outside Whiteladies in December 1984 for Ghostbusters. The Duchess of Beaufort opened the city's oldest surviving cinema Whiteladies in November 1921. Built by a consortium of local businessmen the cinema seated 1300 people and boasted an elegant restaurant and dance hall. In the 1930 it was sold to ABC in a package that also included the Clifton Triangle cinema and the Beau Nash in Bath. In November 2000 it was threatened with closure for the second time in two years due to falling attendances and the opening of multiplex cinemas at St Philips, Hengrove and Cribbs Causeway. Its future is still in the balance.

Pupils from Redland Junior School and St John's Primary School, Keynsham, act the part of wartime evacuees for the launch of the play The Day War Broke Out In Bristol. The 60-strong cast, all in period costume, arrived at Temple Meads on the 1012hrs from Keynsham, the town where the community play was created. May 1995.

November 1993. The most famous Reliant Robin three-wheeler of all time is put under wraps by a BBC crew at the end of a day's filming. Bristol was being used for location filming for an Only Fools And Horses Christmas special. Filming brought with it some temporary changes as street signs were switched. Brunswick Square became Brunswick Square SE15, Southwark Council. The square had previously been used by the Beeb for location filming for the drama series House of Elliot.

1973 marked the 600th anniversary of the founding of the City and County of Bristol. The BBC joined in the festivities by staging a round the then popular International It's A Knockout on the Downs. Above: Great Britain appears to be neck-and-neck with Germany in the Maiden in Distress game. Below: Are Great Britain heading for the early bath?

Bristol's Christmas water carnival was finally sunk in 1997: due to lack of sponsorship. The 1996 carnival nearly foundered when the City Council withdrew funding, but it was saved when Courage stepped in at the last minute with an offer to pay for the lights.

Bob-a-Job week comes to the Hippodrome in April 1987.
Taking a breather from their light dusting are lads of the
Avon Scout Council. The roof opened (it still does) to let
in fresh air.

Fireworks on a grand scale during the 125th anniversary celebrations for the Clifton Suspension Bridge, designed by Brunel in 1830, but not finished until 1864, five years after his death.

and Royal Portbury, both Portishead and the Floating Harbour have been redeveloped and gentrified. Portbury, completed in 1977, is capable of handling ships of up to 120,000tonnes. Gordano Quay was equipped to handle container traffic, a massive gantry crane for loading and unloading ships and Hyster forklifts for stacking operations.

Despite its facilities Portbury found it difficult to attract sufficient traffic to warrant a dedicated container wharf and diversified into other bulk cargoes. Gordano Quay now handles softwood, paper products and general cargo. River Quay handles bulk coal traffic and animal feed, St George's Quay is where bulk gypsum is landed as well as 250,000 motor vehicles a year.

Well into the 1960s it looked as though the City Docks would continue to handle coastal and short-sea traffic. With this in mind modernisation and upgrading continued with the installation of new electric cranes at Wapping Railway Wharf and over at Princes Wharf, Western Fuels felt confident enough to install new rail-fed coal drops. Trade however fell away. The last commercial cargo handled at Wapping Wharf was in 1974 when a consignment of timber Baltic was discharged. Western Fuels closed their depot in 1989. During the period covered in this book Bristol's shipbuilding industry all but came to an end with the closure of the Albion Yard. However in 1979 David Abel opened a small yard specialising in workboats, riverboats and the like.

At Avonmouth a new 30,000tonne capacity granary was built in the mid-1960s, expanding the port's grain storage facilities by 50%. But one of the most lucrative contracts to come to the port was that of Geest Line. For no less than 24 years Geest Line had been using Barry Dock in South Wales for its weekly banana traffic from the West Indies. By the early 1980s Geest were supplying about 40 per cent of the UK demand for bananas, each ship bringing in a cargo of 3200tonnes, or about 20million bananas. The company were a major customer at Barry, their business worth millions of pounds a year to the port. Port of Bristol negotiators spent a year convincing Geest to switch to Avonmouth.

Geest rightly demanded that even during dock disputes their ship's perishable cargoes would be discharged and cleared from Avonmouth. This agreement was considered essential in order to protect the economy of the Windward Islands, which earned just about all its income from bananas. In return the Geest contract in effect guaranteed continuous employment for 70 of Avonmouth's dockers.

In March 1987 the Port of Bristol won yet another important cargo service when the UK West Africa conference, a consortium of ten shipping lines, began sending ships to Avonmouth. The news coincided with launch of a roll-on roll-off container service between the port and Bulgaria.

Giving us a passable performance as the African Queen, the iron-hulled drag-boat BD6 hard at work in August 1961. Built by the Bristol Iron Foundry, Cheese Lane, in 1843, she was designed by Brunel to remove accumulations of mud from quay walls and lock gates. She wasn't broken up until 1964, though her engine and main winch gear are preserved.

Taken in June 1974. This is the Holms Sand & Gravel depot that used to grace Bathurst Basin. In the background stands Bristol General Hospital. Sand dredgers finally vacated the old city docks in 1990, leaving the old Poole's Wharf in Hotwell to be re-developed for up-market housing.

The Bathurst Basin bascule bridge in raised position.
Constructed in 1872 it carried both road and rail traffic.
Though it no longer exists it is still possible to see two
short lengths of mixed broad and standard gauge railway
track in situ near the Ostrich pub.

17th April 1954. Queen Elizabeth and the Duke of Edinburgh arrive at Bristol by sea. The Queen was in the city to officially open the newly completed Council House at College Green. The picture was taken at Broad Quay.

Canons Marsh, August 1954. It was here that cargoes of woodpulp used to be landed for use by St Anne's Board Mills. Note the busy scene as the docks railway steam train pulls away.

The Canon's Marsh tobacco-bond warehouses were substantial if somewhat drab affairs, rarely warranting more than a casual glance from anyone passing by. However they turned out to be Bristol's star attraction on the day they were demolished with explosives. Now you see them. Now you don't.

Now one of Bristol's principal tourist attractions, the
SS Great Britain is seen here externally restored to
something approaching her appearance when she was
completed in 1843.

Brunel's SS Great Britain back in Bristol: in the very same purpose-built dock where she had been built and from where she had been launched. Following her return from the Falklands, she was opened to the public for the first time on 22 July 1970: there were 30,000 visitors in the first twelve days.

The Bristol Sand terminal (Holms Sand & Gravel Co) at Hotwells. This picture was taken in December 1983, by which time the sand dredger Sand Sapphire was the largest commercial vessel making regular use of the Floating Harbour, and the terminal was on the hit list as gentrification of the docks gathered momentum.

The Mardyke ferry carried 300 people a day between Hotwell Road and Spike Island.
It was the last of the old boat links across Bristol harbour. In April 1962 it was
announced that the ferry was to close: axed because it was operating at a loss of
£900 a year,but it managed to struggle on for the next ten years.

Classic action from the Albion Yard in April 1965 as the dredger William Cooper slides down the way. It was however a worrying time at the shipyard. The only other work on hand was a partly completed suction dredger for the Port of Bristol Authority: the order book was empty and the yard's 700 workers were facing an uncertain future.

The end of an era as the last ship to be built at Hill's shipyard takes to the water. The Miranda Guinness, a 1541tonne tanker, wasn't the maximum size of vessel that could be built at the yard. By increasing both the length and reducing the gradient of the ways, Hills were theoretically able to tender for coastal tankers, tugs, dredgers, sludge hoppers and so on up to about 3500tonnes. However by the mid 1970s the company was finding it increasingly more difficult to compete and decided to call it a day. The yard finally closed in 1977.

Washday for Mrs Perry at No2 Old Dock Cottages, Cumberland Basin. January 1958.

19 June 1967. P & A Campbell's Bristol Channel excursion vessel Westward Ho! awaits her turn to enter Cumberland Basin. The swing bridge is open to allow a German registered coaster into the docks. Despite its size and weight, the bridge is turned by just two 60hp electric motors. In the event of a national grid power failure, the bridge is equipped with an emergency generator. However, during the long hot summer of 1976 the bridge jammed askew due to heat expansion and had to be cooled with jets of water.

Following her laying up in September 1966, Campbells received a number of enquiries about the Cardiff Queen. Eventually she was sold in January 1968 for use as a floating night club at Newport. The project bombed before it got started with resulting in Cardiff Queen being sold to John Cashmore for breaking up. She is seen here at Cashmore's Newport yard alongside the rapidly diminishing remains of the anti-submarine frigate HMS Ursa.

A train heads for Portishead while across the river a P & A Campbell excursion steamer stands alongside the Hotwells landing stage. The raked funnels, sweep of the bow, white-painted bridge and additional lifeboats on the aft deck, suggest that she is Campbell's one and only Bristol Queen. Built by Charles Hill & Sons in 1946, she was specially designed for long-distance excursion services.

July 1970. CJ King's diesel tug Sea Alert assists with the hulk of Brunel's Great Britain. Along with the tugs John King and Talgarth she was assigned to towing the Great Britain from Avonmouth to the Cumberland Basin. Built in 1960 Sea Alert was King's first modern tug. Some years later she was sold to Irish owners and then to Labrador Marine Services. In March 1996 the Evening Post carried a report that she had been lost with all hands off Labrador.

Owned by shipbuilders Charles Hill & Sons, the Bristol City Line operated services between Avonmouth, New York and Montreal. The opening of the St Lawrence enabled the company to extend its service into the Great Lakes. One of their ships, the Toronto City was the first ocean-going cargo ship to dock at Milwaukee.

The tug Bristolian takes the strain astern of the China Mutual Steam Navigation Co's Mark A2 class cargo liner Autolycus. The liner was one of six sisters built for Alfred Holt & Co for use on the pilgrim traffic between the Far East and Jeddah. They were fitted out with 'tween deck accommodation, additional sanitary and toilet areas and extra lifeboats. The picture was taken in October 1964, by which time Autolycus had been stripped of her pilgrim capacity and was employed on normal scheduled CMSN Co services.

Bristol Steam Navigation Co container sisterships Apollo and Echo alongside 'N' berth
at Avonmouth. Between them the two ships operated services to Dublin (three sailings
weekly) and Cork (one sailing weekly).

July 1978. The port authority shows off its newly installed traffic control system for the regulating of shipping movements in, out and around Avonmouth.

During the early months of 1984 Avonmouth was crippled by industrial disputes. A walk-out by lock gatemen was followed by a series of strikes by dockers over pay and a management imposed ban on overtime just added to the problems. The Geestbay had docked on Sunday 5th February to discharge 20million bananas, take on an export cargo and sail the following Thursday. Because of the disruption she wasn't expected to finish discharging until the 14th at the earliest, forcing Geest Line to divert the Geest Star to Barry. It just so happened that Geest had only recently abandoned using Barry in favour of Avonmouth.

May 1974. Excavation work for the West Dock (Royal Portbury) is progressing.

David Neale, assistant engineer on the West Dock project, takes a look at the massive pillars supporting the River Quay. The picture was taken in November 1975 when the dock was only half full of water. When fully flooded the pillars would be totally submerged.

The square-rigged ship Lord Nelson visited Bristol in May 1994. Owned by the Jubilee
Trust, she had been adapted so that disabled people could sail on her and take an
active part in working her. She left Bristol; for a five-day cruise to Brixham, Devon,
with a crew of fifty including ten disabled people.

The Floating Harbour and Canons Marsh in 1995.
Showing the distinctive circular shape of the Lloyds
Bank H.Q, the first new development on the marsh.

The Plimsoll Bridge is the
largest swingbridge in the
UK: the construction of
which used 60,000tonnes of
concrete and 3600tonnes of
steel. It also happens that
the streetlights on the
approach roads are thought
to be the tallest in Britain.

Visitors watch a demonstration of the method that use to be used during the days of sail to get vessels into Bristol. Here the Matthew is being assisted by towboats, the number used depending upon river and weather conditions and the size of the ship needing assistance.

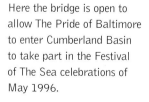

Here the bridge is open to allow The Pride of Baltimore to enter Cumberland Basin to take part in the Festival of The Sea celebrations of May 1996.

A busy scene on Princes Wharf during the Festival of The Sea 1996. The paddle steamer Waverley doubles as a floating grandstand as visitors watch one of the events taking place in the Floating Harbour. Built by A & J Inglis of Glasgow for the London & North Eastern Railway, Waverley is the UK's last sea-going paddle steamer.

Avonmouth 1993.

The massive New Forest Products warehouses at Royal Portbury. Constructed 1995-96, they are used for the storage of linerboard, wood pulp and so on.

The replica of Cabot's ship, the Matthew, was one of the highlights of the Festival of The Sea. Designed by naval architect Colin Mudie: work began on her in February 1994 when her keel of Oepepe, an African hardwood, was laid down on the dockside at Redcliffe Wharf. Opepe was used simply because no oak or elm of sufficient length or quality could be located anywhere in the UK. Much of the oak used in the rest of her construction came from trees blown down at Longleat during the storms of 1990.

Final preparations are underway at Royal Portbury in May 1993 to unload the port's first shipment of coal. The Ascension had arrived with 30,000tonnes of American coal, the discharge of which was to be used to test the unloading equipment and the conveyor system that would carry the coal under the Avon to a railhead at Avonmouth.

The Harry Brown heading out to the Bristol Channel to dredge for yet another load of building sand – a task she performed every day of the year for nearly thirty years.

A credit to the hours and hours of hard work that has gone into and continues to go into the restoration of the SS Great Britain. This is the restored first-class dining saloon.

Luxury 1840s style. Fund raising assistant Catherine Bollard tries out one of the restored cabins for size. Less than six feet long, the cabin is fitted out with two bunks and a washstand: there was some storage space for trunks.

The West Dock, 25 June 1976.

This is what the West Dock (Royal Portbury) might well have looked like had the Arab-Israeli Six Day War not got in the way. With the Suez Canal out of action, ships sailing to and from UK ports, West Africa, India, the Far East and Australia, were faced with the long haul around Southern Africa. This led to a radical rethink in ship design and cargo handling. Supertankers, bulk carriers, container ships and specialist handling and storage facilities were the result.

Registered dockers push their black books forward: if it's taken, they have work. Winning the Geest contract from Barry guaranteed regular work for 70 men every week.

26th February 1977. The German coaster Edith Sabban makes history, becoming the first vessel to officially enter Portbury. Her cargo was a £1.3million gantry crane manufactured in Belgium for handling containers. The crane was erected on Gordano Quay but was to see little service. Despite the introduction of a UK-Canada service in 1980, the port failed to attract sufficient container traffic and quickly turned its attentions to other bulk cargoes.

The heavy mob at work. The Grimstad registered Uglen was brought in to lift two cranes onto a barge for delivery to a North Sea oil platform. Each lift was 193.5tonnes.

Crowds of onlookers gathered at Portishead Point in 1994 to watch no less than six tugs bring the 122,000tonne Greek registered tanker Captain Veniamis into Royal Portbury. Not only was t a race against the tide; the tanker was the biggest vessel ever to enter Bristol. Portbury lock, the largest in the UK, is 140ft wide, the beam of the Captain Veniamis 134ft.

Portishead Dock in June 1973. The town's power station is still active as is Albright & Wilson's chemical works. Today (2002) the picture is very different. With shipping concentrated on Avonmouth and Royal Portbury, the Portishead dock area is being redeveloped at an estimated cost of £400million. Some 3500 homes are to be built, along with a new primary school, bars, restaurants and a retail centre. Moorings for 450 boats will also be provided.

One of Leif Hoegh's car carriers waiting to unload several thousand cars vehicles at Royal Portbury. These purpose-built ships are known as PCTCs (pure car and truck carriers).

Albright & Wilson's Valetta registered Bright Pioneer arrives at Portishead with yet another cargo of liquid phosphorous from the firm's facility in Newfoundland. In July 1982 Bright Pioneer was in the news when it was announced that she was to undertake a round-the-world voyage, delivering phosphorous to Malaysia and Japan. The return leg would take her through the Panama Canal, returning to Portishead via Newfoundland.

The P & A Campbell paddle steamer Britannia seen here towards the end of her career. She was the last survivor of three near-sisters built between 1894 and 1896. She underwent an extensive refit in 1948, being given a new boiler, fitted for oil-firing and given a second funnel. From the autumn of 1949 Campbells put her to work on their Bristol Channel services, principally the Cardiff-Ilfracombe service. Expensive to operate, she fell victim to Campbell cost-cutting and was withdrawn at the end of the 1956 season and sold for breaking up.

In Defence of The Realm

It is impossible to cover this topic in great depth, space simply doesn't allow it. So we have concentrated on a few areas that are immediately identifiable with Bristol during the last fifty years. Mainly HMS Bristol, the Glorious Glosters and 501 (City of Gloucester) Squadron Royal Auxiliary Air Force, but also the RNR drillship Flying Fox as well as visiting warships and army units.

Completed in 1972 HMS Bristol, the seventh warship to carry the name, was the first, and only, Type 82 destroyer to be built. Designed as air defence escorts for a new generation of aircraft carriers, there were to have been nine Bristols, but they were cancelled along with the carriers.

The only three-funnelled ship in the Royal Navy, she was also the first to carry the Sea Dart GWS30 SAM guided missile system. During the Falklands Conflict she was one of half-a-dozen Sea Dart equipped ships deployed to provide the fleet with air defence cover. In later years she combined her role as an operational warship with that of training ship for young naval officers and engineering apprentices. In June 1991 she arrived at Avonmouth for a last visit to Bristol prior to decommissioning.

In its 300-year history the Gloucestershire Regiment (28th/61st Foot) had amassed more battle honours than any other regiment in the British Army. The unique back badge, worn on the back of their hats, honoured the regiment's action at the Battle of Alexandria in 1801 where it fought back-to-back to beat off French attacks from front and rear. During the Korean War the regiment found further fame, when at Imjin it made an heroic stand against overwhelming odds: for which it was awarded the United States Presidential Citation. That citation is represented by affixing a streamer of blue silk to the regiment's Colours. Surviving the amalgamations of the 1950s and 60s, the Glosters became a victim of the Options for Change of the 1990s and were amalgamated with the Duke of Edinburgh's Royal Regiment.

1957 was a disastrous year for the Royal Auxiliary Air Force, the insane decision having been taken to disband all flying squadrons. After giving the nation 27 years of distinguished service 501 paraded on Sunday 3rd February, to be officially disbanded before the Duke of Gloucester.

Flying Officer John Crossley however mounted a one-man protest, taking off in a Vampire without authorisation. Crossley ignored visual signals to land and the fact that he wasn't wearing a flying helmet meant that he was out of radio contact. He flew along the Avon Gorge at around 500mph, passing underneath the Suspension Bridge with just nine or ten feet to spare.

Unfortunately he lost control whilst attempting a victory roll and crashed. He was buried with full military honours.

Set high above the entrance of Dorset House is a crest underneath which is one word – Gibraltar. Since 1949 this grand building in Litfield Place, Clifton, had been the local headquarters for Bristol's Royal Marine reservists. In April 1990 the MOD announced that the unit would soon be moving to a new home that this stately pile would be offered for sale.

April 1959. The RNR drillship Flying Fox is eased from her moorings for a short trip across the river to dry dock for a refit. A veteran of the Great War in which she had served as a minesweeping sloop, Flying Fox was reconstructed for use as a drillship in the early 1920s. She served until 1972 when the unit moved to a purpose-built shore establishment.

In January 1943 the Royal Navy ordered 46 long-range submarines specifically designed for the war against Japan. These new A class submarines were the first boats in the RN to have an all-welded hull, an air-warning radar capable of working at periscope depth and the relatively high surface speed of 18.5 knots. The overall length was 280.5ft; surface displacement 1385tonnes; Submerged displacement 1620tonnes. The first of the class, HMS Amphion, was laid down at Vickers, Barrow in November 1943. Launched in August 1944 only she and HMS Astute were completed before the end of hostilities. Thirty of the class were cancelled. This picture was taken in June 1954 when Amphion paid a visit to Bristol.

HMS Exmouth at Bristol in October 1975. This Blackwood class anti-submarine frigate was the first warship in the world to be powered by gas turbines, being converted in 1966 in a project involving Bristol-Siddeley Engines Ltd. Her power plant, a marine version of aircraft jet engines, comprised a Bristol-Siddeley Olympus rated at 22500shp for high-speed operations and two Proteus gas turbines rated at 3250shp each for normal cruising. Exmouth's auxiliaries were powered by a gas turbine developed by Centrax.

Smiles all round as HMS Bristol returns intact from the Falklands. During the conflict, Sea Dart missiles fired from Bristol and five similarly equipped Sheffield class destroyers are thought to have brought down eight hostile aircraft. More importantly however was the fact that these medium height missiles forced the Argentinian pilots to change tactics and launch their attacks at low altitude, resulting in the failure of many of their bombs to arm after being dropped.

HMS Bristol. One of the lessons learned by the Royal Navy during the Falklands was the fact that there was still nothing like getting some lead into the air. Known these days as CIWS, close-in weapons systems, Bristol's anti-aircraft armament was enhanced with the fitting of two twin GCM-A03-2 Oerlikon amidships and two 1000rpm 20mm GAM-B01 mounts aft.

The Glorious Glosters parade at Bristol to be granted the Freedom of the City – the right to march through with bayonets fixed, drums beating and colours flying. In 1948 the two regular battalions were amalgamated to form a new 1st Battalion (28TH/61ST Foot) and until the formation through amalgamation of large infantry regiments in the 1960s, the Glosters carried more battle honours on their Colours than any other regiment in the Army.

Members of the 1st Battalion the Glorious Gloster on foot patrol in Northern Ireland in 1978.

On one occasion when the Glosters paraded at Castle Park to exercise the regiment's Freedom of the City, they found themselves with an addition to the ranks. Christine Prosser, aged six, and armed only with her mum's umbrella, copied the drill movements to the delight of the crowd. Her mum later told the 'Post' that Christine had had a little help from the sergeant on the end of the rank. "He explained to her how to stand at ease and at one stage she saluted him and he saluted her back – the crowd were in fits." Entering into the spirit of moment Lt-Col Paul Arengo-Jones turned a blind eye to the antics of his newest recruit.

The band of the Wessex Regiment plays the Kynegad Slashers as it leads the farewell parade of the Glorious Glosters. With a history stretching back some 300 years, the Glosters had amassed 141 battle honours. However, under the Options for Change, history counted for little. The Glosters had been one of a handful of regiments to have escaped the amalgamations of earlier years, but now, in March 1994, they were to merge with the Duke of Edinburgh's Royal Regiment to form the Royal Gloucestershire, Berkshire & Wiltshire Regiment.

Avon's reserve forces gather around The Centre in August 1977 in advance of a visit to the city by Queen Elizabeth.

Practice makes perfect. Members of the 6th (TA) Battalion Light Infantry, rehearse an eyes right. The battalion had been selected to provide the guard of honour for the forthcoming visit by the Queen. August 1977.

It is July 1955 and 501 Squadron are off to work on their tans with a summer camp on Gibraltar. Here Squadron-Leader M C Collings briefs his pilots prior to departure. After taking off four of the jets did a farewell flypast over Filton.

501 (City of Gloucester) Squadron, Royal Auxiliary Air Force, recruited in the Bristol area. The squadron's De Haviland Vampires are seen here lined up at RAF Tangmere during the unit's summer camp in July 1953. The squadron hold the Second World War distinction of being the last RAF combat unit to be withdrawn from France after Dunkirk.

The wreckage of Flying Officer Crossley's Vampire jet, Avon Gorge, 3 February 1957. Crossley had been attempting a victory roll under the Clifton Suspension Bridge when he crashed. He was just 28 years old.

A Tornado puts in an appearance at Filton during the celebrations held by Rolls Royce to mark 75 years of aero-engine production at the plant. A display of Bristol-engined aircraft past and present included a Fairey Swordfish, Bristol Blenheim, Jaguar and a Harrier. September 1995.